POETRY 1
Readings

Mike Torbe *a n d* Don Fry

Hodder & Stoughton

LONDON SYDNEY AUCKLAND TORONTO

Cover illustrator: Irene Wise

British Library Cataloguing in Publication Data
Poetry readings 1.
 1. Poetry in English. Anthologies
 I. Fry, Donald II. Torbe, Mike
 821.008

 ISBN 0 340 52416 2

First published 1990

Typeset by Wearside Tradespools, Fulwell, Sunderland
Printed for the educational publishing division of Hodder and Stoughton Ltd, Mill Road, Dunton Green, Sevenoaks, Kent by St. Edmundsbury Press Ltd, Bury St. Edmunds, Suffolk

Contents

Acknowledgments   viii

Introduction   ix

1. 'Miracle on St David's Day', Gillian Clarke (b.1937)   1
   Anthology: 'My Box'   5
              'Baby-Sitting'   6
              'Marged'   6
   Suggestions for assignments   7

2. 'As the Team's Head-Brass', Edward Thomas
   (1878–1917)   8
   Anthology: From *The Diary of Edward Thomas*   12
              From *The Great War and Modern Memory*,
                  Paul Fussell   12
              From *Death's Men*, Denis Winter   14
              From *Diary of Wilfred Owen*   15
              From *World Without End*, Helen Thomas   16
   Suggestions for assignments   18

3. 'Digging', Seamus Heaney (b.1939)   21
   Anthology: 'Ogun', Edward Kamau Brathwaite   24
              'Swami Anand', Sujata Bhatt   25
   Suggestions for assignments   26

4. 'Half-caste', John Agard (b.1949)   28
   Anthology: 'As Others See Us', Basil Dowling   32

'Pity for Poor Africans', William Cowper 32
'My Name', Magoleng wa Selepe 34
'Foreign', Carol Ann Duffy 35
'Epilogue', Grace Nichols 35
Suggestions for assignments 36

5. 'A Roadside Feast', Peter Redgrove (b.1932) 37
Anthology: 'The Crabs', Richard Lattimore 39
'The Trout', John Montague 39
'Finding a Sheep's Skull', Frances Horovitz 40
Suggestions for assignments 41

6. 'A Poison Tree', William Blake (1757–1827) 43
Anthology: 'The Sick Rose' 46
'The Garden of Love' 47
'London' 48
Suggestions for assignments 49

7. 'A Night Piece', William Wordsworth (1770–1850) 50
Anthology: From *The Grasmere Journals*, Dorothy
Wordsworth 54
'The Cock is Crowing', William Wordsworth 54
From *The Grasmere Journals*, Dorothy
Wordsworth 55
'Daffodils', William Wordsworth 56
Suggestions for assignments 57

8. 'Buffaloes', Sujata Bhatt (b.1956) 58
Anthology: 'That Distance Apart (*Part V*)', Jackie Kay 62
'When I Heard the Learn'd Astronomer',
Walt Whitman 62
'The Coming of Good Luck', Robert
Herrick 63
Suggestions for assignments 63

9. 'During Wind and Rain', Thomas Hardy (1840–1928)   64
   Anthology: '"Ah, Are You Digging on My Grave?"'   72
   'Birds at Winter Nightfall'   73
   'Faintheart in a Railway Train'   73
   'The Frozen Greenhouse'   73
   'The Photograph'   74
   'The Voice'   75
   'The Woman in the Rye'   75
   Suggestions for assignments   76

10. 'Travelling Through the Dark', William Stafford (b.1914)   77
    Anthology: 'Enemy Encounter', Padraic Fiacc   80
    'Interruption to a Journey', Norman
    MacCaig   81
    'Mouse's Nest', John Clare   81
    Suggestions for assignments   82

Acknowledgments

The Publishers and authors would like to thank Sally Ingham at Settlebeck School, Sedbergh, and Libby Gurr and the English Department at the Holt School, Wokingham, for their invaluable advice on early drafts of this manuscript.

The Publishers would like to thank the following for permission to reproduce material in this volume:

Anvil Press Poetry for 'Foreign' by Carol Ann Duffy from *Selling Manhattan* (1987); The Black Staff Press for 'Enemy Encounter' by Padraic Fiacc; Carcanet Press Ltd for 'Baby Sitting', 'My Box', 'Miracle on St David's Day' and 'Marged' from *Selected Poems* by Gillian Clarke (1985), 'Buffaloes' and 'Swami Anand' from *Brunizem* by Sujata Bhatt and two extracts from *World Without End* by Helen Thomas; Faber and Faber Ltd for 'Digging' from *Death of a Naturalist* by Seamus Heaney; The Hogarth Press Ltd for 'Interruption to a Journey' by Norman MacCaig from *Collected Poems*; John Montague for 'The Trout'; Newstatesman Society for 'A Roadside Feast' by Peter Redgrove; Oxford University Press for extracts from *The Great War and Modern Memory* by Paul Fussell (1975) and 'Ogun' from *The Arrivants* by Edward Kamau Brathwaite (1973); Penguin Books Australia Ltd for 'As others see us' by Basil Dowling from Alan Curnow (ed) *Penguin Book of New Zealand Poetry*; William Stafford for his poem 'Travelling through the Dark' from *Stories That Could Be True*; Virago Press for 'Epilogue' by Grace Nichols from *The Fat Black Woman's Poems* (1984).

Every effort has been made to trace and acknowledge ownership of copyright. The publishers will be glad to make suitable arrangements with any copyright holders whom it has not been possible to contact.

The Publishers would also like to thank the following for permission to reproduce photographs and illustrations:

Hulton Picture Company (pages 8 (top) and 13); Barnaby's Picture Library (pages 8, 9 and 15); Borde na Mona (page 21); the illustrations on pages 44, 46, 47, 48 reproduced by the courtesy of the Trustees of the British Museum; the Bridgeman Art Library for 'The Clearing in the Forest' by Caspar-David Friedrich on page 50; Robert Harding Picture Library (page 59).

Introduction

R eading poetry is rarely easy. Even experienced readers are
uncertain when they read a new poem for the first time, so it is
not surprising that inexperienced readers should often find
poetry difficult.

This series of books introduces readers to different ways of reading
poems to show that even poems which at first look difficult can be
explored and understood. The approaches are as active as possible so
that readers examine meanings in many different ways. Book One is
intended for students in the earlier stages of reading poetry.

Each book is divided into ten units, and each unit contains:

- a core poem with its exploratory work

- an anthology

- some suggestions for assignments.

The units are arranged alphabetically by the first line of the poem, and
could be taken in any order that seems appropriate. They are of
different lengths, depending on the poem and the approaches it
suggests.

Each core poem is dealt with in a sequence of activities which have
been designed to lead students through a process of making meaning.
Some activities come before the poem and prepare the reader for the
first reading; others come afterwards and aim to help readers
understand and feel comfortable with different aspects of the poem's
form, language and, above all, its meaning.

The poems in the anthologies sometimes have a theme similar to that
of the main poem, sometimes are other poems by the same writer, and
sometimes reflect varying aspects of the main poem in the unit. Readers
can browse through the anthologies and speculate about the
connections; they might also sometimes make up their own anthologies
to go with the core poem.

The 'Suggestions for Assignments' offer ideas for oral and written work, which could be supplemented or replaced by a teacher's or the student's own suggestions. All assignments have to recognise the unpredictable nature of individual interests, and there should always be room for people to construct their own topics, and for individuals and groups to work at their own pace.

Students and teachers will need to decide how long to spend on a unit, and what can be done in class and what in the students' own time. Not all students, for example, will want to follow the core poem through to an assignment, and sometimes it might be better to work on the anthology later in the course.

We assume that groups have access to a library, dictionaries and other reference books to do research about poets and to find the meanings of words. Often, though, *people* are the best resource: asking questions, of each other and of helpful and informed people, will probably supply answers to many problems.

We expect that this book would represent only part of the work on poetry in a class. There would also be a general browsing through anthologies and collections, people writing their own poetry, individuals making their own choices of poems and devising assignments, visits from poets themselves to read their poems, and poetry having a place in other units of work.

1

Gillian Clarke

MIRACLE ON ST DAVID'S DAY

'They flash upon that inward eye
Which is the bliss of solitude'
'The Daffodils' by W. Wordsworth

An afternoon yellow and open-mouthed
with daffodils. The sun treads the path
among cedars and enormous oaks.
It might be a country house, guests strolling,
the rumps of gardeners between nursery shrubs.

I am reading poetry to the insane.
An old woman, interrupting, offers
as many buckets of coal as I need.
A beautiful chestnut-haired boy listens
entirely absorbed. A schizophrenic

on a good day, they tell me later.
In a cage of first March sun a woman
sits not listening, not seeing, not feeling.
In her neat clothes the woman is absent.
A big, mild man is tenderly led

to his chair. He has never spoken.
His labourer's hands on his knees, he rocks
gently to the rhythms of the poems.
I read to their presences, absences,
to the big, dumb labouring man as he rocks.

He is suddenly standing, silently,
huge and mild, but I feel afraid. Like slow
movement of spring water or the first bird
of the year in the breaking darkness,
the labourer's voice recites 'The Daffodils'.

1

The nurses are frozen, alert; the patients
seem to listen. He is hoarse but word-perfect.
Outside the daffodils are still as wax,
a thousand, ten thousand, their syllables
unspoken, their creams and yellows still.

Forty years ago, in a Valleys school,
the class recited poetry by rote.
Since the dumbness of misery fell
he has remembered there was a music
of speech and that once he had something to say.

When he's done, before the applause, we observe
the flowers' silence. A thrush sings
and the daffodils are flame.

This poem tells a story. There are things the poet doesn't tell us in the poem:

- whether she's been here before
- why she's doing this
- what the inside of the mental hospital looked like to her
- how she felt when she saw the patients
- what she saw when she looked around her
- what she thought when the old woman interrupted her
- how she felt about the audience as she was reading
- why she felt afraid when the man stood up
- what she did while the man was reciting
- what happened afterwards
- what she and the nurses talked about after the reading was finished
- what difference the whole experience has made to her

▷ Write a story called 'Miracle on St David's Day', using the poem, and adding to it your solutions to the problems above.

▷ Did the daffodils play an important part in your story? How do they matter in the poem?

It's a true story, and I told it many times before I found a way to write the poem. The occupational therapist of a mental hospital invited me to read poems to the patients on the first of March, St David's Day. It was a beautiful spring afternoon, and daffodils lit the lawns about the occupational therapy centre, which stood among trees apart from the main building.

There were about fifteen patients present. Some listened alertly, others were so blank and still that I could sense the silence behind their eyes, and a few interrupted me, thinking they were somewhere else.

Walter, the dumb man, was a Council workman suffering from a depression so profound that he had lost the power of speech, though there was nothing physically wrong with him. Long ago, when he was a child in one of the coal-mining valleys of South Wales, where education was very highly regarded, he and his class-mates had learned poems by heart, as they had learned their tables and many other things. He was suddenly reminded of Wordsworth's poem, and his silence was unlocked.

The poem is about the power of language, especially poetry. Our minds are full of voices, and our bodies – tongues, ears, hands, feet – love sound and rhythm. Poetry is easier to memorise than prose, and its works of art are free and can be carried anywhere and turned to in the loneliest moments – in hospital, in prison, in exile.

At first I tried to write a poem about voices speaking out of silence – silent daffodils, silent patients, a thrush singing, a dumb man speaking. The poem failed, draft after draft. At last I just told the story, setting the scene with three sentences of description. I chose every word carefully – the 'open-mouthed' afternoon, the sun 'treading' the path, the people 'observing' the silence of the flowers. 'Observing' has at least two meanings here. The woman 'in a cage' sat where the grid-pattern of sunlight fell, but her cage is also her illness.

Indoors the people were 'frozen' and silent. Outside the natural world was singing and dancing like 'flame'. We see, think and speak. We take this for granted, and the words within us meet the world outside and express our relationship with it. These ill people suffered from a disconnection between thought and language. The abyss within was more real to them than the beautiful world just outside their window.

To succeed, a poem needs a writer and a reader, a speaker and a listener. For one miraculous moment Walter listened, and he spoke. Language had done its healing work, and what was inside him, and the real, outside world of spring sunlight, daffodils, thrushes, lawn-mowers and people walking in the gardens, were reconnected through a poem.

GILLIAN CLARKE

MY BOX

My box is made of golden oak,
my lover's gift to me.
He fitted hinges and a lock
of brass and a bright key.
He made it out of winter nights,
sanded and oiled and planed,
engraved inside the heavy lid
in brass, a golden tree.

In my box are twelve black books
where I have written down
how we have sanded, oiled and planed,
planted a garden, built a wall,
seen jays and goldcrests, rare red kites,
found the wild heartsease, drilled a well,
harvested apples and words and days
and planted a golden tree.

On an open shelf I keep my box.
Its key is in the lock.
I leave it there for you to read,
or them, when we are dead,
how everything is slowly made,
how slowly things made me,
a tree, a lover, words, a box,
books and a golden tree.

BABY-SITTING

I am sitting in a strange room listening
For the wrong baby. I don't love
This baby. She is sleeping a snuffly
Roseate, bubbling sleep; she is fair;
She is a perfectly acceptable child.
I am afraid of her. If she wakes
She will hate me. She will shout
Her hot midnight rage, her nose
Will stream disgustingly and the perfume
Of her breath will fail to enchant me.

To her I will represent absolute
Abandonment. For her it will be worse
Than for the lover cold in lonely
Sheets; worse than for the woman who waits
A moment to collect her dignity
Beside the bleached bone in the terminal ward.
As she rises sobbing from the monstrous land
Stretching for milk-familiar comforting,
She will find me and between us two
It will not come. It will not come.

MARGED

I think of her sometimes when I lie in bed,
falling asleep in the room I have made in the roof-space
over the old dark parlŵr where she died
alone in winter, ill and penniless.
Lighting the lamps, November afternoons,
a reading book, whisky gold in my glass.
At my type-writer tapping under stars
at my new roof-window, radio tunes
and dog for company. Or parking the car
where through the mud she called her single cow
up from the field, under the sycamore.
Or looking at the hills she looked at too.
I find her broken crocks, digging her garden.
What else do we share, but being women?

Marged is the name of the person who used to live in this house in
Wales before the writer came there. Parlŵr is Welsh for parlour.

Suggestions for assignments ─────────────

1 Using the material in this unit, write a piece on Gillian Clarke, introducing her to new readers. Describe the sorts of things she chooses to write about, how she writes about them, and the kind of person she seems to be. Use extracts from the poems to show what you mean.

2 Write answers to these questions about the poems in the anthology:
My Box: What does the poem tell us about Gillian Clarke's life and what she values?
Baby-Sitting: The babysitter says 'I am afraid of her'. What makes her afraid?
Marged: Why is Gillian Clarke so interested in the person who used to live here before she did?

2

Edward Thomas

It is 1917, in Gloucestershire. A ploughman is ploughing a field which has lain fallow. There is a wood along one side of it, and a tree has fallen at the opposite side from the wood. Sitting on the fallen tree is a man in uniform, who watches the ploughman, and also sees two people just going into the wood. The horses pulling the plough have head-brasses which the soldier sees flash in the sun as they turn at the end of the furrow and come back up towards him.

When the plough turns near the soldier, the ploughman rests and chats to him. Then he sets off again, with the earth turning over away from the blade of the plough-share.

The ploughman explains how the tree fell. The soldier asks when they'll move it, the ploughman answers, and so they chat, during the one minute out of every ten that the plough is resting near the soldier. The soldier speaks first and the conversation turns to the war. In France, men are dying, guns are firing, trenches are being dug, and the Great War is destroying the youth of Europe. But here, the soldier takes his last look at the peaceful scene before he leaves it.

Here now is the poem, 'As the Team's Head-Brass'. Edward Thomas, the poet, who is the soldier in the poem, did go to war. He was killed in Flanders in 1917.

AS THE TEAM'S HEAD-BRASS

As the team's head-brass flashed out on the turn
The lovers disappeared into the wood.
I sat among the boughs of the fallen elm
That strewed the angle of the fallow, and
Watched the plough narrowing a yellow square
Of charlock. Every time the horses turned
Instead of treading me down, the ploughman leaned
Upon the handles to say or ask a word,
About the weather, next about the war.
Scraping the share he faced towards the wood,
And screwed along the furrow till the brass flashed once more.
           The blizzard felled the elm whose crest
I sat in, by a woodpecker's round hole,
The ploughman said. 'When will they take it away?'
'When the war's over.' So the talk began –
One minute and an interval of ten,
A minute more and the same interval.
'Have you been out?' 'No.' 'And don't want to, perhaps?'
'If I could only come back again, I should.
I could spare an arm. I shouldn't want to lose
A leg. If I should lose my head, why, so,
I should want nothing more. . . . Have many gone
From here?' 'Yes.' 'Many lost?' 'Yes, a good few.
Only two teams work on the farm this year.
One of my mates is dead. The second day
In France they killed him. It was back in March,
The very night of the blizzard too. Now if
He had stayed here we should have moved the tree.'
'And I should not have sat here. Everything
Would have been different. For it would have been
Another world.' 'Ay, and a better, though
If we could see all all might seem good.' Then
The lovers came out of the wood again:
The horses started and for the last time
I watched the clods crumble and topple over
After the ploughshare and the stumbling team.

▷ Make a sketch or diagram of the scene in the poem, showing the field, the tree, the wood, the characters, the movement of the ploughing team, and so on.

▷ Think of the poem as bringing together three worlds:

- the world of the soldier
- the world of the ploughman
- the world of war

Make a copy of this diagram big enough for you to write in the circles.

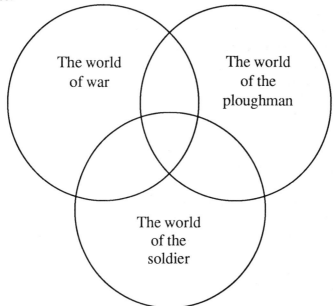

Where in this diagram would you place these elements from the poem:

- the fallen tree
- the ploughman's mate
- the blizzard
- the lovers
- the ploughing

Which did you find the hardest to decide about?

▷ Explain why you put the elements where you did. You could do this either as a piece of writing, or as notes for a presentation to the rest of the class.

11

20th. Stiff deep mud all the way up and shelled as we started. Telegraph Hill as quiet as if only rabbits lived there. I took revolver and left this diary behind in case. For it is very exposed and only a few Cornwalls and MGC [Machine Gun Corps] about. But Hun shelled chiefly over our heads into Beaurains all night – like starlings returning 20 or 30 a minute. Horrible flap of 5.9 a little along the trench. Rain and mud and I've to stay till I am relieved tomorrow. Had not brought warm clothes or enough food and had no shelter, nor had telephonists. Shelled all night. But the M.G.C. boy gave me tea. I've no bed. I leant against wall of trench. I got up and looked over. I stamped up and down. I tried to see patrol out. Very light – the only sign of Hun on Telegraph Hill, though 2 appeared and were sniped at. A terribly long night and cold. Not relieved till 8. Telephonists out repairing line since 4 on the morning of the . . .

21st. At last 260 relieved us. Great pleasure to be going back to sleep and rest. No Man's Land like Goodwood Racecourse with engineers swarming over it and making a road between shell holes full of blood-stained water and beer bottles among barbed wire. Larks singing as they did when we went up in dark and were shelled. Now I hardly felt as if a shell could hurt, though several were thrown about near working parties. Found letters from Helen, Eleanor and Julian. Had lunch, went to bed at 2 intending to get up to tea, but slept till 6.30 on the [22nd]

(*Diary of Edward Thomas*)

Since dawn was the favourite time for launching attacks, at the order to stand-to everyone, officers, men, forward artillery observers, visitors, mounted the fire-step, weapon ready, and peered toward the German line. When it was almost full light and clear that the Germans were not going to attack that morning, everyone 'stood down' and began preparing breakfast in small groups. The rations of tea, bread, and bacon, brought up in sandbags during the night, were broken out. The bacon was fried in mess-tin lids over small, and if possible smokeless, fires.

(*The Great War and Modern Memory* by Paul Fussell)

The agony of the men being shelled began well before the explosion. The skilled ear picked out each gun, noted its calibre, the path of its shell and the likely explosion point. The small field gun went off with a crack like a fat man hitting a golf ball. The shell took off like a jet plane and arrived with a screaming shriek. A keen pair of eyes might pick out the fifteen-foot gunflash, blinding even as a flashlight in daytime. The medium artillery piece sounded like a giant newspaper being torn, its shell a farmcart coming down a steep hill with its brakes on. The heavy gun rapped a man's head with a heavy cane then rolled in a leisurely arc across the sky, a man on a bicycle whistling slowly and pensively. For a time the listener felt he could run beside it. Then it speeded up like an express train rushing down a tunnel. Shells passing over woods and valleys echoed. Shells falling in enclosed places came with a double bang and no warning. A near miss would whistle or roar, with debris raining down long after the burst. The strain of listening for all these sounds did something to the brain. A man could never be rid of them. [. . .]

If a man were unstable and ill-suited to war, whatever he might consciously think, a shellburst would most effectively prick the lie. Drury remembered an eighteen-year-old trembling for twenty-four hours after a dud dropped ten yards from him.

(*Ibid.*)

Birds gave pleasure to most. The bared soil rich in nitrates from shelling and free from the attention of farmers produced a vast crop of plants, particularly of cornflowers and poppies. Attracting insects, these flowers brought birds in their wake. A letter in the *Daily Express* (27 October 1918) noted sixty species within two miles of Péronne. The resilience of these birds gave men hope, and the press published a succession of letters, like *The Times* (2 March 1916), which noted a nightingale nesting in the front line at Hooge. A nightingale sang on the Ancre three days after a mustard attack (16 June 1918) with comment from the *Guardian*. The *Daily Express* (5 May 1916) published a letter describing a blackbird laying four eggs and bringing up its young in the guts of a heavy gun in constant use. However harsh the barrage, birds never missed the dawn chorus.

(*Death's Men* by Denis Winter)

We had a march of 3 miles over shelled road then nearly 3 along a flooded trench. After that we came to where the trenches had been blown flat out and had to go over the top. It was of course dark, too dark, and the ground was not mud, not sloppy mud, but an octopus of sucking clay, 3, 4, and 5 feet deep, relieved only by craters full of water. Men have been known to drown in them. Many stuck in the mud & only got on by leaving their waders, equipment, and in some cases their clothes.

(Diary of Wilfred Owen)

Today the Somme is a peaceful but sullen place, unforgetting and unforgiving. The people, who work largely at raising vegetables and grains, are 'correct' but not friendly. To wander now over the fields destined to extrude their rusty metal fragments for centuries is to appreciate in the most intimate way the permanent reverberations of July, 1916. When the air is damp you can smell rusted iron everywhere, even though you see only wheat and barley. The farmers work the fields without joy. They collect the duds, shell-casings, fuses, and shards of old barbed wire as the plow unearths them and stack them in the corners of their fields. Some of the old barbed wire, both British and German, is used for fencing. Many of the shell craters are still there, though smoothed out and grown over. The mine craters are too deep to be filled and remain much as they were. When the sun is low in the afternoon, on the gradual slopes of the low hills you see the traces of the zig-zag of trenches. Many farmhouses have out in back one of the little British wooden huts that used to house soldiers well behind the lines; they make handy toolsheds. Lurking in every spot of undergrowth just off the beaten track are eloquent little things: rusted buckles, rounds of corroded small-arms ammunition, metal tabs from ammunition boxes, bits of Bully tin, buttons.

(The Great War and Modern Memory)

Thomas's wife wrote about herself ('Jenny') and Thomas. Here are two extracts from her book.

The days had passed in restless energy for us both. He had sawn up a big tree that had been blown down at our very door, and chopped the branches into logs, the children all helping. The children loved being with him, for though he was stern in making them build up the logs properly, and use the tools in the right way, they were not resentful of this, but tried to win his rare praise and imitate his skill. Indoors he packed his kit and polished his accoutrement. He loved a good piece of leather, and his Sam Browne and high trench-boots shone with a deep clear lustre. The brass, too, re-minded him of the brass ornaments we had often admired when years ago we had lived on a farm and knew every detail of a plough team's harness. We all helped with the buttons and buckles and badges to turn him out the smart officer it was his pride to be. For he entered into this soldiering which he hated in just the same spirit of thoroughness of which I have spoken before. We talked, as we polished, of those past days: 'Do you remember when Jingo, the grey leader of the team, had colic, and Turner the ploughman led her about Blooming Meadow for hours, his eyes streaming with tears because he thought she was going to die? And how she would only eat the hay from Blooming Meadow, and not the coarse hay that was grown in Sixteen Acre Meadow for the cows? And do you remember Turner's whip which he carried over his shoulder when he led Darling and Chestnut and Jingo out to the plough? It had fourteen brass bands on the handle, one for every year of his service on the farm.' So we talked of old times that the children could remember.

(*World Without End* by Helen Thomas)

'And here are my poems. I've copied them all out in this book for you, and the last of all is for you. I wrote it last night, but don't read it now.... It's still freezing. The ground is like iron, and more snow has fallen. The children will come to the station with me; and now I must be off.'

We were alone in my room. He took me in his arms, holding me tightly to him, his face white, his eyes full of a fear I had never seen before. My arms were round his neck. 'Beloved, I love you,' was all I could say. 'Jenny, Jenny, Jenny,' he said, 'remember that, whatever happens, all is well between us for ever and ever.' And hand in hand we went downstairs and out to the children, who were playing in the snow.

A thick mist hung everywhere, and there was no sound except, far away in the valley, a train shunting. I stood at the gate watching him go; he turned back to wave until the mist and the hill hid him. I heard his old call coming up to me: 'Coo-ee!' he called. 'Coo-ee!' I answered, keeping my voice strong to call again. Again through the muffled air came his 'Coo-ee'. And again went my answer like an echo. 'Coo-ee' came fainter next time with the hill between us, but my 'Coo-ee' went out of my lungs strong to pierce to him as he strode away from me. 'Coo-ee!' So faint now, it might be only my own call flung back from the thick air and muffling snow. I put my hands up to my mouth to make a trumpet, but no sound came. Panic seized me, and I ran through the mist and the snow to the top of the hill, and stood there a moment dumbly, with straining eyes and ears. There was nothing but the mist and the snow and the silence of death.

Then with leaden feet which stumbled in a sudden darkness that overwhelmed me I groped my way back to the empty house.

(Ibid.)

Suggestions for assignments

1 Here is the beginning of the conversation in the poem printed as though it were a page from a play:

SOLDIER: When will they take it away?
PLOUGHMAN: When the war's over.
            (There is a pause during which the plough moves away and then returns.)

Work with another person and try different ways of acting out the conversation between the soldier and the ploughman.

As you decide how they would speak, you will have to think of their state of mind.

Remember that the way people feel sometimes comes out in the way they say things, but sometimes what they really feel isn't shown.

What are you going to do about the pauses?

Now go back to the poem on page 10.

Decide how the two of you will read the poem aloud. When you are ready, record or perform your reading to others.

2 The poem tells you what the soldier sees, what he says, and what he does. What is he feeling though? What is he thinking?

Think of yourself as the soldier. Describe what he sees, says and does in the course of the poem, and add to it your description of what he feels and thinks. Use 'I' and write as though the events are happening now.

3 Use the poem, and all the anthology material. Imagine one of these scenes:

(a) It's dawn, and the soldier in the poem is at the Front.
(b) The soldier has returned home and revisits the place in the poem.
(c) The wife receives a letter from the Front.

You could write in any of these forms:

- a conversation
- a diary
- a story
- a letter or an exchange of letters
- a poem
- memoirs written many years later

3

Seamus Heaney

▷ Write the word 'digging' in the middle of a piece of paper. Work together and write down whatever comes into your mind about the word. Write your suggestions around the paper in whatever way seems best.

'Digging' was Seamus Heaney's first published poem. The poet hears the sound of a spade, as his father works in the garden outside the room where the poet is writing. He remembers his own childhood twenty years ago, and his father working in the potato field. 'By God,' he thinks, 'the old man could handle a spade, just like his old man,' (i.e. his own grandfather). He remembers taking milk to his grandfather, while he was cutting turf for burning.

DIGGING

Between my finger and my thumb
The squat pen rests; snug as a gun.

Under my window, a clean rasping sound
When the spade sinks into gravelly ground:
My father, digging. I look down

Till his straining rump among the flowerbeds
Bends low, comes up twenty years away
Stooping in rhythm through potato drills
Where he was digging.

The coarse boot nestled on the lug, the shaft
Against the inside knee was levered firmly.
He rooted out tall tops, buried the bright edge deep
To scatter new potatoes that we picked
Loving their cool hardness in our hands.

By God, the old man could handle a spade.
Just like his old man.

My grandfather cut more turf in a day
Than any other man on Toner's bog.
Once I carried him milk in a bottle
Corked sloppily with paper. He straightened up
To drink it, then fell to right away

Nicking and slicing neatly, heaving sods
Over his shoulder, going down and down
For the good turf. Digging.

The cold smell of potato mould, the squelch and slap
Of soggy peat, the curt cuts of an edge
Through living roots awaken in my head.
But I've no spade to follow men like them.

Between my finger and my thumb
The squat pen rests.
I'll dig with it.

▷ There are three generations mentioned in the poem. Mark on a copy of the poem the parts which are about each of them. One way is to put different coloured boxes round the various bits.

▷ Make a note of when the words 'dig' or 'digging' are used in the poem, and which lines they are in.
   Who is doing the 'digging' in each case?

▷ Go back to the word web you made for 'digging'. Now that you know that the word is the title of this poem, cross out the words that no longer seem to fit.
   What different meanings does the word 'digging' have in the poem?

▷ On another piece of paper, draw a box and write in it one sentence about the poem. It could be a question you want to ask, a statement you want to make about the poem's meaning to you, or something it has made you remember or think about.
   Exchange papers within your group, and write comments on each others' versions.
   When you get your own paper back, revise or add to your original boxed statement in the light of what other people have said, and what you have read.

Seamus Heaney has written that when he was writing the poem 'Digging', he remembered something said by an old roadman he knew as a child. He would pass the man on his way to school and make himself late by talking to him. The man's job was to cut back the brambles and tidy up the verge. Heaney writes:

Leaning on his spade, this man once said to me: 'The pen's easily handled. It's a lot lighter than the spade. Aye, boy, it's lighter than the spade, I'm telling you.'

▷ 'But I've no spade . . .'
   Why does he say that? Is he ashamed of it, or pleased and relieved?

23

OGUN

My uncle made chairs, tables, balanced doors on, dug out
coffins, smoothing the white wood out

with plane and quick sandpaper until
it shone like his short-sighted glasses.

The knuckles of his hands were sil-
vered knobs of nails hit, hurt and flat-

tened out with blast of heavy hammer. He was knock-knee'd, flat-
footed and his clip clop sandals slapped across the concrete

flooring of his little shop where canefield mulemen and a fleet
of Bedford lorry drivers dropped in to scratch themselves and talk.

There was no shock of wood, no beam
of light mahogany his saw teeth couldn't handle.

When shaping squares for locks, a key hole
care tapped rat tat tat upon the handle

of his humpbacked chisel. Cold
world of wood caught fire as he whittled: rectangle

window frames, the intersecting x of fold-
ing chairs, triangle

trellises, the donkey
box-cart in its squeaking square.

But he was poor and most days he was hungry.
Imported cabinets with mirrors, formica table

tops, spine-curving chairs made up of tubes, with hollow
steel-like bird bones that sat on rubber ploughs,

thin beds, stretched not on boards, but blue high-tensioned cables,
were what the world preferred.

And yet he had a block of wood that would have baffled them.
With knife and gimlet care he worked away at this on Sundays,

explored its knotted hurts, cutting his way
along its yellow whorls until his hands could feel

how it had swelled and shivered, breathing air,
its weathered green burning to rings of time,

its contoured grain still tuned to roots and water.
And as he cut, he heard the creak of forests:

green lizard faces gulped, grey memories with moth
eyes watched him from their shadows, soft

liquid tendrils leaked among the flowers
and a black rigid thunder he had never heard within his hammer

came stomping up the trunks. And as he worked within his shattered
Sunday shop, the wood took shape: dry shuttered

eyes, slack anciently everted lips, flat
ruined face, eaten by pox, ravaged by rat

and woodworm, dry cistern mouth, cracked
gullet crying for the desert, the heavy black

enduring jaw; lost pain, lost iron;
emerging woodwork image of his anger.

EDWARD KAMAU BRATHWAITE

SWAMI ANAND

In Kosbad during the monsoons
there are so many shades of green
your mind forgets other colours.

At that time
I am seventeen, and have just started
to wear a sari every day.
Swami Anand is eighty-nine
                and almost blind.
His thick glasses don't seem to work,
they only magnify his cloudy eyes.
Mornings he summons me
        from the kitchen
and I read to him until lunch time.

One day he tells me
'you can read your poems now'
I read a few, he is silent.
Thinking he's asleep, I stop.
But he says, 'continue'.
I begin a long one
in which the Himalayas rise
                    as a metaphor.
Suddenly I am ashamed
to have used the Himalayas like this,
ashamed to speak of my imaginary mountains
to a man who walked through
            the ice and snow of Gangotri
                    barefoot
a man who lived close to Kangchenjanga
        and Everest clad only in summer cotton.
I pause to apologize
but he says 'just continue'.

Later, climbing through
            the slippery green hills of Kosbad,
Swami Anand does not need to lean
on my shoulder or his umbrella.
I prod him for suggestions,
ways to improve my poems.
He is silent a long while,
then, he says
            'there is nothing I can tell you
                except continue.'

SUJATA BHATT

Suggestions for assignments _____

1 One concern of the poems in this section is memories about events in
the poets' lives, concerning people from an older generation whom the
poets respect, and from whom they learnt something important.

Write about your own memories of some older person who seems
now to be important to you.
Notice what the three poems do:

- They are very precise about the place.

- They give physical details of clothing, tools and belongings.

- They give strong pictures of the people. (You might want to use
  photographs of the person you are writing about.)

- They make it very clear what the older people were good at.

2 Suppose we said to each of the poets, Why have you written about these people? Examples of the questions you could ask are:

- What is it about your father and grandfather/your uncle/the Swami that you especially remember?
- Do you feel you are different from them?
- What difference did they make to your life and your work?
- What did you mean when you said 'as he cut [my uncle] heard the creak of forests'?
- How did you feel when the Swami said 'There is nothing I can tell you except continue'?
- What do you three poets feel you have in common?

Some of the ways you could organise this would be to:

- work on your own and write the answers as a report of an interview
- work with a partner and prepare an interview which you could record or present to the class
- work as a whole class, with each poet played by a different person

The oral part of this assignment could lead to written work which could either be a transcript of the interview, or an essay.

4

John Agard

In the book *The Heart of the Race*, a woman describes being at a conference where there was a discussion of mixed race. She says:

> A lot of women there were angry about terms like 'half-caste' and 'coloured' because they saw them as being divisive. When you think about it, even the word sounds like a put down, like 'half-done' ... As far as I'm concerned, I'm a *Black* woman, because I live that reality.
>
> (*The Heart of the Race* by Beverley Bryan)

John Agard, originally from Guyana, describes himself as

> Me not no Oxford don,
> me a simple immigrant
> from Clapham Common
> I didn't graduate
> I immigrate

In the next poem, John Agard writes about 'half-caste' in ways that force readers to ask what the phrase actually means. (The poem continues over the page, on page 30.)

HALF-CASTE

Excuse me
standing on one leg
I'm half-caste

Explain yuself
wha yu mean
when yu say half-caste
yu mean when picasso
mix red an green
is a half-caste canvas/
explain yuself
wha yu mean
when yu say half-caste
yu mean when light an shadow
mix in de sky
is a half-caste weather/
well in dat case
england weather
nearly always half-caste
in fact some o dem cloud
half-caste till dem overcast
so spiteful dem dont want de sun pass
ah rass/
explain yuself
wha yu mean
when yu say half-caste
yu mean tchaikovsky
sit down at dah piano
an mix a black key
wid a white key
is a half-caste symphony/

Explain yuself
wha yu mean
Ah listening to yu wid de keen
half of mih ear
Ah lookin at yu wid de keen
half of mih eye
an when I'm introduced to yu
I'm sure you'll understand
why I offer yu half-a-hand
an when I sleep at night
I close half-a-eye
consequently when I dream
I dream half-a-dream
an when moon begin to glow
I half-caste human being
cast half-a-shadow
but yu must come back tomorrow

wid de whole of yu eye
an de whole of yu ear
an de whole of yu mind

an I will tell yu
de other half
of my story

▷ Read the poem aloud. Work in pairs and try it in different ways:

- as though you are angry with another person

- as though you are having a polite conversation

- as though you are having a debate

- as though you are trying to understand what another person feels

- as though you are making fun of the person who is using the words

Did one of these readings feel easier to do?

▷ Work in pairs and study the language in which this poem has been deliberately written, looking especially at these things:

- forms of Standard English used (e.g. 'Excuse me')

- non-standard spelling (e.g. 'yu, yuself')

- non-standard grammar (e.g. 'england weather')

- punctuation
- repetition of words, structures and other patterns (e.g. 'Explain yuself . . .')

List examples under those headings, and make notes of anything else you notice.

What kind of English is the poem written in?

Why did John Agard choose to write it the way he did?

▷ Here are the final seven lines of the poem rewritten in Standard English:

> but you must come back tomorrow
>
> with the whole of your eye
> and the whole of your ear
> and the whole of your mind
>
> and I will tell you
> the other half
> of my story

What difference does it make if the poem is written like this?

▷ People may have very different feelings about the word 'half-caste'. List arguments explaining why it is or is not a good title for the poem.

Working in pairs, construct an argument, with one person saying 'half-caste' is a bad title and another saying it is a good title. You can either do this orally, or in a piece of writing.

In this poem a man knows that he is hiding his real self from the world.
The writer was a white New Zealander.

AS OTHERS SEE US

With 'No Admittance' printed on my heart,
    I go abroad, and play my public part;
And win applause – I have no cause to be
    Ashamed of that strange self that others see.

But how can I reveal to you, and you,
    My real self's hidden and unlovely hue?
How can I undeceive, how end despair
    Of this intolerable make-believe?

You must see with God's eyes, or I must wear
    My furtive failures stark upon my sleeve.

BASIL DOWLING

The next poem was written at the time when England was involved in
the slave trade.

PITY FOR POOR AFRICANS

Video meliora proboque,
Deteriora sequor.

I own I am shock'd at the purchase of slaves,
And fear those who buy them and sell them are knaves;
What I hear of their hardships, their tortures, and groans,
Is almost enough to draw pity from stones.

I pity them greatly, but I must be mum,
For how could we do without sugar and rum?
Especially sugar, so needful we see;
What, give up our desserts, our coffee, and tea!

Besides if we do, the French, Dutch, and Danes
Will heartily thank us, no doubt, for our pains;
If we do not buy the poor creatures, they will;
And tortures and groans will be multiplied still.

If foreigners likewise would give up the trade,
Much more in behalf of your wish might be said;
But, while they get riches by purchasing blacks,
Pray tell me why we may not also go snacks?

Your scruples and arguments bring to my mind
A story so pat, you may think it is coin'd,
On purpose to answer you, out of my mint;
But I can assure you I saw it in print.

A youngster at school, more sedate than the rest,
Had once his integrity put to the test;
His comrades had plotted an orchard to rob,
And ask'd him to go and assist in the job.

He was shock'd, sir, like you, and answer'd, 'Oh no!
What! rob our good neighbour? I pray you don't go!
Besides, the man's poor, his orchard's his bread:
Then think of his children, for they must be fed.'

'You speak very fine, and you look very grave,
But apples we want, and apples we'll have;
If you will go with us, you shall have a share,
If not, you shall have neither apple nor pear.'

They spoke, and Tom ponder'd – 'I see they will go;
Poor man! what a pity to injure him so!
Poor man! I would save him his fruit if I could,
But staying behind will do him no good.

'If the matter depended alone upon me,
His apples might hang till they dropp'd from the tree;
But since they will take them, I think I'll go too;
He will lose none by me, though I get a few.'

His scruples thus silenced, Tom felt more at ease,
And went with his comrades the apples to seize;
He blamed and protested, but join'd in the plan;
He shared in the plunder, but pitied the man.

WILLIAM COWPER

The author of the following poem is a Black South African.

MY NAME

Nomgqibelo Ncamisile Mnqhibisa

Look what they have done to my name . . .
the wonderful name of my great-great-grandmothers
Nomgqibelo Ncamisile Mnqhibisa

The burly bureaucrat was surprised.
What he heard was music to his ears
'Wat is daai, sê nou weer?'
'I am from Chief Daluxolo Velayigodle of emaMpodweni
And my name is *Nomgqibelo Ncamisile Mnqhibisa*.'

Messia, help me!
My name is so simple
and yet so meaningful,
but to this man it is trash . . .

He gives me a name
Convenient enough to answer his whim:
I end up being
Maria . . .
I . . .
Nomgqibelo Ncamisile Mnqhibisa.

MAGOLENG WA SELEPE

34

The writer of this piece was born in Glasgow.

FOREIGN

Imagine living in a strange, dark city for twenty years.
There are some dismal dwellings on the east side
and one of them is yours. On the landing, you hear
your foreign accent echo down the stairs. You think
in a language of your own and talk in theirs.

Then you are writing home. The voice in your head
recites the letter in a local dialect; behind that
is the sound of your mother singing to you,
all that time ago, and now you do not know
why your eyes are watering and what's the word for this.

You use the public transport. Work. Sleep. Imagine one night
you saw a name for yourself sprayed in red
against a brick wall. A hate name. Red like blood.
It is snowing on the streets, under the neon lights,
as if this place were coming to bits before your eyes.

And in the delicatessen, from to time, the coins
in your palm will not translate. Inarticulate,
because this is not home, you point at fruit. Imagine
that one of you says *Me not know what these people mean.*
It like they only go to bed and dream. Imagine that.

CAROL ANN DUFFY

Grace Nichols was born in Guyana and came to the UK in 1977.

EPILOGUE

I have crossed an ocean
I have lost my tongue
from the root of the old one
a new one has sprung

GRACE NICHOLS

Suggestions for assignments

1 Write something of your own to go with the poems in this anthology. Decide where you want to place your writing in the sequence, and whether it will be one long piece or several shorter pieces.

2 You have already done some work on the language of the John Agard poem, which you could now write up.

Look at the language of the other poems in the way you studied the language of John Agard's poem. Some questions you could ask yourself are:

- Why does Grace Nichols write in Standard English?

- How would you describe William Cowper's English?

- Why are there different languages in Selepe's poem?

3 The issues raised in this unit are about people's freedom to be themselves. Write an essay about this question:

How does language help or prevent people being themselves?

Look at the way the different poems presented here give different answers to that question. Also include your own experiences and those of your friends.

5

Peter Redgrove

A ROADSIDE FEAST

He slaps the hedgehog off the road
He chivvies it off with scraping prongs
He pins it alive on metal points
The blood catches the starlight
He says you must watch for fleas and not touch the vermin
He prods it down in the bank of clay
He stirs it round until it is an earth ball
Taking a twig he scrapes it off
Into the heart of the fire where it glows
And sizzles like a speeding cannonball
A high-pitched cry of juice from a blowhole
With his trowel he dibbles it out on a stone
Taps it and cracks it, the clay shards-off
He pulls them with scalding fingers
A roasting smell pays attention, we lean forward,
Like a six-inch pig the naked food
Glorious with grease. He waves us off
Bake your own hedge-pig, he says.
I pick up a shard, daggered with long pins.

▷ Work out in pairs precisely what happens to the hedgehog in the
poem.
    Could you do what 'he' does?
    Why does 'he' do it?

▷ We watch what happens, but we don't seem to be told how 'I' feels. Work in small groups and complete this chart. Write in the appropriate quotation from the poem.

What happens	Quotation	What 'I' feels
When the blood comes		
When they hear the hedgehog baking		
When the clay comes off the baked hedgehog		
	Bake your own hedge-pig	
	I pick up a shard, daggered with long pins	

▷ Consider these alternative endings, and discuss what difference they would make to the poem.

1: The poem ends with the previous line:
Bake your own hedge-pig, he says.

2: The poem ends with a new last line:
I watch him eat, and turn away.

3: The poem ends with these two lines:
I pick up a shard, daggered with long pins
and the baked clay crumbles in my hand.

THE CRABS

There was a bucket full of them. They spilled,
crawled, climbed, clawed: slowly tossed
and fell: precision made: cold iodine color of their own
world of sand and occasional brown weed, round stone
chilled clean in the chopping waters of their coast.
One fell out. The marine thing on the grass
tried to trundle off, barbarian and immaculate and to be
   killed
with his kin. We lit water: dumped the living mass
in: contemplated tomatoes and corn: and with the good
   cheer of civilized man,
cigarettes, that is, and cold beer, and chatter,
waited out and lived down the ten-foot-away clatter
of crabs as they died for us inside their boiling can.

RICHARD LATTIMORE

THE TROUT

Flat on the bank I parted
Rushes to ease my hands
In the water without a ripple
And tilt them slowly downstream
To where he lay, light as a leaf,
In his fluid sensual dream.

Bodiless lord of creation
I hung briefly above him
Savouring my own absence
Senses expanding in the slow
Motion, the photographic calm
That grows before action.

As the curve of my hands
Swung under his body
He surged, with visible pleasure.
I was so preternaturally close
I could count every stipple
But still cast no shadow, until

39

The two palms crossed in a cage
Under the lightly pulsing gills.
Then (entering my own enlarged
Shape, which rode on the water)
I gripped. To this day I can
Taste his terror in my hands.

JOHN MONTAGUE

FINDING A SHEEP'S SKULL

Sudden shock of bone
at the path's edge,
like a larger mushroom
almost hidden by leaves.

I handle the skull gently
shaking out earth and spiders.
Loose teeth chock in the jaw:
it smells of nothing.

I hold it up to sunlight,
a grey-green translucent shell.
Light pours in
        like water
through blades and wafers of bone.
        In secret caves
filaments of skull hang down;
frost and rain have worked
        to shredded lace.

The seasons waste its symmetry.
        It is a cathedral
echoing spring; in its decay
        plainsong of lamb
        and field and sun
inhabits bone.

The shallow cranium
fits in my palm

– for speculative children
I bring it home.

FRANCES HOROVITZ

Suggestions for assignments _____

1 How does each of the anthology poems remind you of 'Roadside Feast'?

2 Choose one of these suggestions to work on:

Roadside Feast: Write a piece which explains the title, and either says why the poem is worth reading or why no one else should read it.
The Crabs: Imagine you are watching this scene. When you feel familiar enough with the poem, describe what you, the watcher, can see, and what you feel. Do this without referring back to the poem so that you will be describing what you think rather than just summarising the poem itself.
The Trout: Choose a few phrases from the poem which you want to write about. Write each phrase and then an explanation of why it interests you.
Finding a Sheep's Skull: Have you found some relic of a creature? Tell your story about it.

6

William Blake

When you have read 'A Poison Tree' for the first time, write down immediately the first impressions you have, whatever they are. You don't have to write in an organised or coherent way. Just record the initial thoughts and feelings you have as soon as you have finished.

A POISON TREE

I was angry with my friend:
I told my wrath, my wrath did end.
I was angry with my foe:
I told it not, my wrath did grow.

And I water'd it in fears,
Night and morning with my tears;
And I sunned it with smiles,
And with soft deceitful wiles.

And it grew both day and night,
Till it bore an apple bright;
And my foe beheld it shine,
And he knew that it was mine,

And into my garden stole
When the night had veil'd the pole:
In the morning glad I see
My foe outstretch'd beneath the tree.

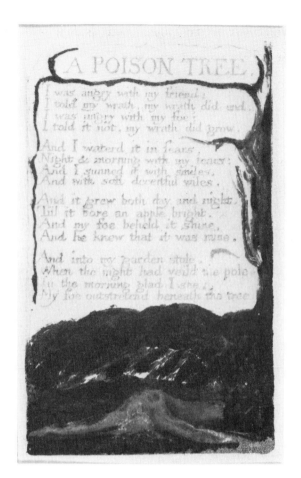

▷ Copy out the poem in pairs of lines. Write underneath each pair whatever the lines make you think of, or, if it seems appropriate, you could include sketches or other artwork. You could set it out like this:

> I was angry with my friend:
> I told my wrath, my wrath did end.

▷ Share what you have done with each other. When you have read other people's versions, write down any questions you have about the poem.

44

▷ What is your view on these ideas? Discuss them with other people.

- You should always express anger.
- It's wrong to be deceitful.
- Your enemy often has things you would like.
- Forgiveness is best.
- Evil things can look very attractive.
- Enemies deserve to be punished.
- It's good to get your own back.
- It's only natural to want revenge.

▷ Write a story, either based on real experience or invented, about a time when you were angry but didn't say so, and about what happened as a result.

THE SICK ROSE

O Rose, thou art sick.
The invisible worm
That flies in the night,
In the howling storm,

Has found out thy bed
Of crimson joy:
And his dark secret love
Does thy life destroy.

THE GARDEN OF LOVE

I went to the Garden of Love,
And saw what I never had seen:
A Chapel was built in the midst,
Where I used to play on the green.

And the gates of this Chapel were shut,
And 'Thou shalt not' writ over the door;
So I turn'd to the Garden of Love,
That so many sweet flowers bore;

And I saw it was filled with graves,
And tomb-stones where flowers should be;
And Priests in black gowns were walking their rounds,
And binding with briars my joys & desires.

LONDON

I wander thro' each charter'd street,
Near where the charter'd Thames does flow,
And mark in every face I meet
Marks of weakness, marks of woe.

In every cry of every Man,
In every Infant's cry of fear,
In every voice, in every ban,
The mind-forg'd manacles I hear.

How the Chimney-sweeper's cry
Every blackning Church appalls;
And the hapless Soldier's sigh
Runs in blood down Palace walls.

But most thro' midnights streets I hear
How the youthful Harlot's curse
Blasts the new-born Infant's tear,
And blights with plagues the Marriage hearse.

Suggestions for assignments ⎯⎯⎯⎯⎯⎯

1 Work with a partner and read the poems together. Study Blake's illustrations, and discuss how the illustrations help you to understand the poems.

Choose one of the poems and find ways of making a picture which represents what you feel about it.

2 Here are some of the titles from Blake's collected *Songs of Innocence and Experience*:

Little Boy Lost
The Chimney Sweeper
Ah Sunflower
Infant Sorrow
The School Boy

Choose one of these and write your own piece – poem or prose – based on the title. Reread the poems in this anthology first, and let your writing be influenced by Blake's work.

7

William Wordsworth

▷ It's night time in a place like the one shown opposite, and the sky is overcast with clouds. There's a full moon, but you can only see it faintly through the clouds.

Write a description of that scene, using these words in your writing:

WHITENED   VEIL   INDISTINCTLY   DULL   LIGHT

▷ There is a traveller walking along the path, deep in thought. There is a break in the clouds, and the sudden brightness makes him look up.

Write a description of the scene, using these words:

GLEAM   STARTLES   UNOBSERVING   SPLIT   GLORY

▷ What does the traveller see as he continues looking up into the night sky?

MULTITUDES   WIND   UNFATHOMABLE   FAST   SILENT

Add a description of how the traveller feels when this moment has passed.

▷ Work your three descriptions into one piece of writing.

Read what other people have written. Choose the bits you like best to read to the rest of the group (or the whole of the class).

How have people used the words 'WHITENED', 'UNFATHOMABLE' and 'FAST'?

▷ What different ways have people used to describe the man's feelings at the end?

Which endings do you like best?

Write an ending together, as a class, using what you like best in each other's versions.

On 25 January 1798, William Wordsworth wrote a poem he called 'A Night-Piece'. He was writing about the scene you have just been recreating.

A NIGHT-PIECE

         – The sky is overcast
With a continuous cloud of texture close,
Heavy and wan, all whitened by the Moon,
Which through that veil is indistinctly seen,
A dull, contracted circle, yielding light
So feebly spread that not a shadow falls,
Chequering the ground – from rock, plant, tree, or tower.
At length a pleasant instantaneous gleam
Startles the pensive traveller while he treads
His lonesome path, with unobserving eye
Bent earthwards; he looks up – the clouds are split
Asunder, – and above his head he sees
The clear Moon, and the glory of the heavens.
There in a black-blue vault she sails along,
Followed by multitudes of stars, that, small
And sharp, and bright, along the dark abyss
Drive as she drives: how fast they wheel away,
Yet vanish not! – The wind is in the trees,
But they are silent; – still they roll along
Immeasurably distant; and the vault,
Built round by those white clouds, enormous clouds,
Still deepens its unfathomable depth.
At length the Vision closes; and the mind,
Not undisturbed by the delight it feels,
Which slowly settles into peaceful calm,
Is left to muse upon the solemn scene.

▷ On a copy of the poem:

- Mark the four sections that match the four pieces of writing you
  did previously.

- Mark words that Wordsworth used that are like words that you
  have used. Has Wordsworth used them in the same way that you
  have?

- Mark any other parts of the poem that remind you of your own
  piece.

▷ The scene is a common one, and yet it seems unusual. Do you
  recognise what Wordsworth describes when he looks up?

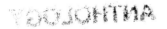

▷   At length the Vision closes; and the mind,
       Not undisturbed by the delight it feels,
       Which slowly settles into peaceful calm,
       Is left to muse upon the solemn scene.

Why did he choose the word 'Vision' rather than a word like 'sight' or 'episode'.

Describe in your own words what is happening in these four lines.

Wordsworth's sister, Dorothy, kept a journal in which she recorded her daily life, including the walks she shared with her brother in the Lake District. The journal was not private, and William and their friends read it. Here is an extract from the journal for 25 January 1798.

> *25th.* The sky spread over with one continuous cloud, whitened by the light of the moon, which, though her dim shape was seen, did not throw forth so strong a light as to chequer the earth with shadows. At once the clouds seemed to cleave asunder, and left her in the centre of a black-blue vault. She sailed along, followed by multitudes of stars, small, and bright, and sharp. Their brightness seemed concentrated, (half-moon).
>
>   (*The Alfoxden Journal*)

▷ Match the extract against Wordsworth's poem. Is there anything that Dorothy writes which William does not use?

ANTHOLOGY

When we came to the foot of Brothers water I left William sitting on the Bridge and went along the path on the right side of the Lake through the wood. I was delighted with what I saw. The water under the boughs of the bare old trees, the simplicity of the mountains and the exquisite beauty of the path. There was one grey cottage. I repeated the Glowworm as I walked along. I hung over the gate, and thought I could have stayed for ever. When I returned I found William writing a poem descriptive of the sights and sounds we saw and heard. There was the gentle flowing of the stream, the glittering lively lake, green fields without a living creature to be seen on them, behind us, a flat pasture with 42 cattle feeding to our left the road leading to the hamlet, no smoke there, the sun shone on the bare roofs. The people were at work ploughing, harrowing and sowing – lasses spreading dung, a dog's barking now and then, cocks crowing, birds twittering, the snow in patches at the top of the highest hills, yellow palms, purple and green twigs on the Birches, ashes with their glittering spikes quite bare. The hawthorn a bright green with black stems under the oak. The moss of the oak glossy. We then went on, passed two sisters at work, they first passed us, one with two pitch forks in her hand. The other had a spade. We had some talk with them. They laughed aloud after we were gone perhaps half in wantonness, half boldness. William finished his poem before we got to the foot of Kirkstone.

(The Grasmere Journals)

THE COCK IS CROWING

The cock is crowing,
The stream is flowing,
The small birds twitter,
The lake doth glitter,
The green field sleeps in the sun;
The oldest and youngest
Are at work with the strongest;
The cattle are grazing,
Their heads never raising;
There are forty feeding like one!

Like an army defeated
The snow hath retreated,
And now doth fare ill
On the top of the bare hill;
The Ploughboy is whooping – anon – anon:
There's joy in the mountains;
There's life in the fountains;
Small clouds are sailing,
Blue sky prevailing;
The rain is over and gone!

When we were in the woods beyond Gowbarrow park we saw a few daffodils close to the water side. We fancied that the lake had floated the seeds ashore and that the little colony had so sprung up. But as we went along there were more and yet more and at last under the boughs of the trees, we saw that there was a long belt of them along the shore, about the breadth of a country turnpike road. I never saw daffodils so beautiful they grew among the mossy stones about and about them, some rested their heads upon these stones as on a pillow for weariness and the rest tossed and reeled and danced and seemed as if they verily laughed with the wind that blew upon them over the lake, they looked so gay ever glancing ever changing. The wind blew directly over the lake to them. There was here and there a little knot and a few stragglers a few yards higher up but they were so few as not to disturb the simplicity and unity and life of that one busy highway. We rested again and again. The Bays were stormy, and we heard the waves at different distances and in the middle of the water like the sea.

(*The Grasmere Journals*)

DAFFODILS

I wandered lonely as a cloud
That floats on high o'er vales and hills,
When all at once I saw a crowd,
A host, of golden daffodils;
Beside the lake, beneath the trees,
Fluttering and dancing in the breeze.

Continuous as the stars that shine
And twinkle on the milky way,
They stretched in never-ending line
Along the margin of a bay:
Ten thousand saw I at a glance,
Tossing their heads in sprightly dance.

The waves beside them danced; but they
Out-did the sparkling waves in glee:
A poet could not but be gay,
In such a jocund company:
I gazed – and gazed – but little thought
What wealth the show to me had brought:

For oft, when on my couch I lie
In vacant or in pensive mood,
They flash upon that inward eye
Which is the bliss of solitude;
And then my heart with pleasure fills,
And dances with the daffodils.

Suggestions for assignments ────────────

1 Many writers and artists make sketches of things they want to remember, and then work on them afterwards to produce a more polished version. William sometimes used Dorothy Wordsworth's journals as his 'notebook', as you have seen, and occasionally used her original words.

Keep a diary for a few days, particularly recording moments that you might want to write about. Record the details that will make the writing as vivid as possible, as Dorothy Wordsworth does. Choose days when you know you will be doing something interesting – going somewhere new, meeting someone and so on.

Leave it for a few days, and then reread the diary and choose one of the entries that you want to write about. Write a poem arising out of your diary entry. Keep all the drafts.

Write a final piece about the whole process. This will include:

- the journal

- the drafts

- the poem

- comments on how you came to write the poem

2 Consider the poems and the extracts from the journals in the anthology.

Write an essay explaining how the two seem to connect with each other and apparently influence each other. Give examples of words and phrases being used in both.

Do you think the poems were written by William, or by William and Dorothy?

8

Sujata Bhatt

▷ Here is a glimpse of a woman. Work together and list as much as you can about her:

- what has happened to her

- where she lives

- how she feels

- what her dreams are

> The young widow
> walks from tree to tree,
> newly opened leaves brush damp sweet smells
> across her face. The infant's mouth sleeps
> against her breast. Dreams stuck
> inside her chest twitch,
> as she watches the buffaloes pass
> too close to her house, up the steep road
> to the dairy.

▷ Here is some more information about her from earlier in the poem.

> The young widow
> thinks she should have burned on
> her husband's funeral pyre.
> She could not, for her mother-in-law
> insisted she raise the only son
> of her only son.
> The young widow sits outside
> in the garden overlooking a large pond.
> Out of the way, still untouchable, she suckles
> her three-week-old son
> and thinks she could live
> for those hungry lips; live to let him grow
> bigger than herself.

Reread your earlier list and adjust what you said there, adding any more information about the woman that you have discovered.

BUFFALOES

The young widow
thinks she should have burned on
her husband's funeral pyre.
She could not, for her mother-in-law
insisted she raise the only son
of her only son.
The young widow sits outside
in the garden overlooking a large pond.
Out of the way, still untouchable, she suckles
her three-week-old son
and thinks she could live
for those hungry lips; live to let him grow
bigger than herself. Her dreams lie
lazily swishing their tails
in her mind like buffaloes
dozing, some with only nostrils showing
in a muddy pond.

Tails switch
to keep fat flies away,
and horns, as long as a man's hand, or longer,
keep the boys, and their pranks away.
It is to the old farmer's tallest son
they give their warm yellowish milk.
He alone approaches: dark-skinned and naked
except for a white turban, a white loincloth.
He joins them in the pond,
greets each one with love:
'my beauty', 'my pet' –
slaps water on their broad flanks
splashes more water on their dusty backs.
Ears get scratched, necks rubbed,
drowsy faces are splashed awake.
Now he prods them out of the mud
out of the water, begging loudly
'Come my beauty, come my pet, let us go!'
And the pond shrinks back
as the wide black buffaloes rise.

The young widow
walks from tree to tree,
newly opened leaves brush damp sweet smells
across her face. The infant's mouth sleeps
against her breast. Dreams stuck
inside her chest twitch,
as she watches the buffaloes pass
too close to her house, up the steep road
to the dairy. The loud loving voice
of the farmer's son holds them steady
without the bite of any stick or whip.

▷ This is a commonplace scene that is repeated in this place often.
Why is it especially important to the young widow today?

▷ What are her dreams about? (lines 13–17 and 42–3).

▷ Imagine a time after the end of this poem, when the young widow
has returned home with her baby, and is talking to someone about
what has happened to her today, and how she feels now. Write your
own piece that begins

The young widow
says —

THAT DISTANCE APART (Part V)

She, my little foreigner
no longer familiar with my womb

kicking her language of living
somewhere past stalking her first words

she is six years old today
I am twenty-five; we are only

that distance apart yet
time has fossilised

prehistoric time is easier
I can imagine dinosaurs

more vivid than my daughter
dinosaurs do not hurt my eyes

nor make me old so terribly old
we are land sliced and torn.

Jackie Kay

WHEN I HEARD THE LEARN'D ASTRONOMER

When I heard the learn'd astronomer,
When the proofs, the figures, were ranged in columns be-
    fore me,
When I was shown the charts and diagrams, to add, divide,
    and measure them,
When I sitting heard the astronomer where he lectured
    with much applause in the lecture-room,

How soon unaccountable I became tired and sick,
Till rising and gliding out I wander'd off by myself,
In the mystical moist night-air, and from time to time,
Look'd up in perfect silence at the stars.

Walt Whitman

THE COMING OF GOOD LUCK

So good luck came, and on my roof did light,
Like noiseless snow, or as the dew of night:
Not all at once, but gently, as the trees
Are by the sunbeams tickled by degrees.

ROBERT HERRICK

Suggestions for assignments _____

1 Take the first draft material you produced in the last task on
'Buffaloes' – writing about 'The young widow says –'. Work it up into a
more polished and final piece which would satisfy readers even if they
had not read the poem.

2 Make a presentation on paper which links the poems together. Put
photocopies of the three anthology poems in the centre of the paper. On
one side write something which describes the feelings at the centre of
the poem. It may help to write this if you begin with 'I realise that . . .'
or 'I feel . . .' or 'I find that . . .'

   On the other side of each poem write something which describes
similar feelings in 'Buffaloes'. You might be able to use some of the
writing you have already done on the poem.

9

Thomas Hardy

Here are four memories of a Victorian family.

1 The family is working together in the garden, clearing and tidying, and making somewhere to sit in the shade:

> They clear the creeping moss –
> Elders and juniors – aye,
> Making the pathways neat
>   And the garden gay;
> And they build a shady seat. . . .

2 In the summer, they breakfast outside. The guinea fowl they keep as pets come up to them for food. In the distance, they can just see the sea:

> They are blithely breakfasting all –
> Men and maidens – yea,
> Under the summer tree,
>   With a glimpse of the bay,
> While pet fowl come to the knee. . . .

3 Another memory is of moving house, with all the furniture out on the lawn, waiting to be loaded on to carts:

> They change to a high new house,
> He, she, all of them – aye,
> Clocks and carpets and chairs
>   On the lawn all day
> And brightest things that are theirs. . . .

4 In the evenings, by candlelight, they all join in singing their favourite songs in harmony, while one person plays the piano:

> They sing their dearest songs –
> He, she, all of them – yea,
> Treble and tenor and bass,
>   And one to play;
> With the candles mooning each face. . . .

▷ Reread each of the four memories. Try picturing each of the memories: you might find it helpful to draw them as though they are photographs in their own frame.

   Put them in some sort of sequence – time of day, time of the year, time of life . . . Which seems the best sequence?

The poem is in four verses, one for each memory. The memories that you have seen end with dots (. . .) meaning that both the memory and the verse are incomplete.

Here are the last two lines of the poem: rain runs down the family gravestone:

> Ah, no; the years, the years;
> Down their carved names the raindrop ploughs.

The poem is called 'During Wind and Rain' and is given over the page as Hardy wrote it.

DURING WIND AND RAIN

They sing their dearest songs –
He, she, all of them, yea,
Treble and tenor and bass,
    And one to play;
With the candles mooning each face. . . .
    Ah, no; the years O!
How the sick leaves reel down in throngs!

They clear the creeping moss –
Elders and juniors – aye,
Making the pathways neat
    And the garden gay;
And they build a shady seat. . . .
    Ah, no; the years, the years;
See, the white storm-birds wing across!

They are blithely breakfasting all –
Men and maidens – yea,
Under the summer tree,
    With a glimpse of the bay,
While pet fowl come to the knee. . . .
    Ah no; the years O!
And the rotten rose is ript from the wall.

They change to a high new house,
He, she, all of them – aye,
Clocks and carpets and chairs
    On the lawn all day,
And brightest things that are theirs. . . .
    Ah, no; the years, the years;
Down their carved names the rain-drop ploughs.

▷ The wind strips the trees, whirls birds across the sky, and tears
down the dead rose. Four times we are reminded of 'the years'
passing.

    Go back to the pictures you drew of the memories. Add
something to them that represents how your view of them has
changed now that you have seen the whole poem.

▷ Work in pairs, and look at the ways in which the poem is patterned. For example:

- look at the sixth line in each verse
- look at the second line in each verse
- look at the words that rhyme with 'play'

Make up some directions of your own that would help other people to discover patterns in the poem.

'AH, ARE YOU DIGGING ON MY GRAVE?'

'Ah, are you digging on my grave,
   My loved one? – planting rue?'
– 'No: yesterday he went to wed
One of the brightest wealth has bred.
"It cannot hurt her now," he said,
   "That I should not be true."'

'Then who is digging on my grave?
   My nearest dearest kin?'
– 'Ah, no: they sit and think, "What use!
What good will planting flowers produce?
No tendance of her mound can loose
   Her spirit from Death's gin."'

'But some one digs upon my grave?
   My enemy? – prodding sly?'
– 'Nay: when she heard you had passed the Gate
That shuts on all flesh soon or late,
She thought you no more worth her hate,
   And cares not where you lie.'

'Then, who is digging on my grave?
   Say – since I have not guessed!'
– 'O it is I, my mistress dear,
Your little dog, who still lives near,
And much I hope my movements here
   Have not disturbed your rest?'

'Ah, yes! *You* dig upon my grave . . .
   Why flashed it not on me
That one true heart was left behind!
What feeling do we ever find
To equal among human kind
   A dog's fidelity!'

'Mistress, I dug upon your grave
   To bury a bone, in case
I should be hungry near this spot
When passing on my daily trot.
I am sorry, but I quite forgot
   It was your resting-place.'

BIRDS AT WINTER NIGHTFALL

(TRIOLET)

Around the house the flakes fly faster,
And a!l the berries now are gone
From holly and cotonea-aster
Around the house. The flakes fly! – faster
Shutting indoors that crumb-outcaster
We used to see upon the lawn
Around the house. The flakes fly faster,
And all the berries now are gone!

FAINTHEART IN A RAILWAY TRAIN

At nine in the morning there passed a church,
At ten there passed me by the sea,
At twelve a town of smoke and smirch,
At two a forest of oak and birch,
    And then, on a platform, she:

A radiant stranger, who saw not me.
I said, 'Get out to her do I dare?'
But I kept my seat in my search for a plea,
And the wheels moved on. O could it but be
    That I had alighted there!

THE FROZEN GREENHOUSE

(ST. JULIOT)

'There was a frost
Last night!' she said,
'And the stove was forgot
When we went to bed,
And the greenhouse plants
Are frozen dead!'

By the breakfast blaze
Blank-faced spoke she,
Her scared young look
Seeming to be
The very symbol
Of tragedy.

The frost is fiercer
Than then to-day,
As I pass the place
Of her once dismay,
But the greenhouse stands
Warm, tight, and gay,

While she who grieved
At the sad lot
Of her pretty plants
Cold, iced, forgot —
Herself is colder,
And knows it not.

THE PHOTOGRAPH

The flame crept up the portrait line by line
As it lay on the coals in the silence of night's profound,
   And over the arm's incline,
And along the marge of the silkworm superfine,
And gnawed at the delicate bosom's defenceless round.

Then I vented a cry of hurt, and averted my eyes;
The spectacle was one that I could not bear,
   To my deep and sad surprise;
But, compelled to heed, I again looked furtivewise
Till the flame had eaten her breasts, and mouth, and hair.

'Thank God, she is out of it now!' I said at last,
In a great relief of heart when the thing was done
   That had set my soul aghast,
And nothing was left of the picture unsheathed from the past
But the ashen ghost of the card it had figured on.

She was a woman long hid amid packs of years,
She might have been living or dead; she was lost to my sight,
   And the deed that had nigh drawn tears
Was done in a casual clearance of life's arrears;
But I felt as if I had put her to death that night! . . .

     .   .   .   .   .   .

— Well: she knew nothing thereof did she survive,
And suffered nothing if numbered among the dead;
   Yet — yet — if on earth alive
Did she feel a smart, and with vague strange anguish strive?
If in heaven, did she smile at me sadly and shake her head?

THE VOICE

Woman much missed, how you call to me, call to me,
Saying that now you are not as you were
When you had changed from the one who was all to me,
But as at first, when our day was fair.

Can it be you that I hear? Let me view you, then,
Standing as when I drew near to the town
Where you would wait for me: yes, as I knew you then,
Even to the original air blue gown!

Or is it only the breeze, in its listlessness
Travelling across the wet mead to me here,
You being ever dissolved to wan wistlessness
Heard no more again far or near?

    Thus I; faltering forward,
    Leaves around me falling,
Wind oozing thin through the thorn from norward,
    And the woman calling.

December 1912

THE WOMAN IN THE RYE

'Why do you stand in the dripping rye,
Cold-lipped, unconscious, wet to the knee,
When there are firesides near?' said I.
'I told him I wished him dead,' said she.

'Yea, cried it in my haste to one
Whom I had loved, whom I well loved still;
And die he did. And I hate the sun,
And stand here lonely, aching, chill;

'Stand waiting, waiting under skies
That blow reproach, the while I see
The rooks sheer off to where he lies
Wrapt in a peace withheld from me!'

Suggestions for assignments ⎯⎯⎯⎯⎯⎯⎯

1 How could you tell that all these poems were written by the same person? Write some notes about any similarities of theme, style and language that you find. Use those notes to prepare a poster that shows the similarities. You can use photocopies of the poems, coloured pens, paste, scissors and anything else that will help.

2 Work in groups and prepare performances of a sequence of some of the poems using appropriate music or pictures. Decide on the best order for the poems you have chosen. You might want to use some of Hardy's poems which you have chosen yourselves from other books. You could include some of your own writing which either puts an alternative view to Hardy's, or is similar in tone and feeling to his.

3 If this was the only evidence you had about Hardy, what would you guess about his life?

Imagine there is a diary by Hardy. Write the extracts from the diary that relate to the poems here.

10

William Stafford

TRAVELLING THROUGH THE DARK

Travelling through the dark I found a deer
dead on the edge of the Wilson River road.
It is usually best to roll them into the canyon:
that road is narrow; to swerve might make more dead.

By glow of the tail-light I stumbled back of the car
and stood by the heap, a doe, a recent killing;
she had stiffened already, almost cold.
I dragged her off; she was large in the belly.

My fingers touching her side brought me the reason –
her side was warm; her fawn lay there waiting,
alive, still, never to be born.
Beside that mountain road I hesitated.

The car aimed ahead its lowered parking lights;
under the hood purred the steady engine.
I stood in the glare of the warm exhaust turning red;
around our group I could hear the wilderness listen.

I thought hard for us all – my only swerving –
then pushed her over the edge into the river.

▷ Do you see pictures when you read? Some people think they see moving pictures, some see still pictures; others say they don't see any pictures at the time, but when they think about it afterwards, they do.

What happens when you and your friends read this poem? Do you see pictures?

▷ Trying to picture this poem is trying to understand it. One way of picturing is creating a storyboard, that is a script for a film or television programme.

A storyboard gives an indication of what images might be used, any voice over, and any music or other sound effects. Lay it out like this.

IMAGE	V/O	FX

Produce a storyboard that could be used in the making of a video of this poem. Begin with the title frame, try to use between ten and fifteen frames, and indicate camera angles, close-ups and long shots. Don't bother about producing beautiful drawings. What matters is that your image should show what you think is most important.

▷ How many people are in your video?
What was your most important close-up?
Which were the silent moments in your storyboard?
Which parts couldn't you make pictures for? Which words or lines of the poem did you have to leave out?

▷ What different endings for the film have been suggested in your group?

Most films wouldn't end where the poem ends. Some possible endings in a film would be:

- The car drives away, silence returns. The camera focuses on the river, and zooms in slowly on the body of the deer.

- We see a close-up of the man. The camera pulls further and further back until he seems just a dot in the landscape in the lights of the car.

- The driver gets back into the car and drives away. We follow and see close-ups of the expression on his face. Then the car drives away from us and we see its tail lights disappearing into the night.

But a film could also end the same way the poem does:

- We see the man push the deer over and the screen goes blank and silent.

Write a description of what you think would be the best way to end the film.

▷　　　　I thought hard for us all – my only swerving –
　　　　then pushed her over the edge into the river.

What is there to think about?

ENEMY ENCOUNTER

for Lilac

Dumping (left over from the autumn)
Dead leaves, near a culvert
I come on
          a British Army Soldier
With a rifle and a radio
Perched hiding. He has red hair.

He is young enough to be my weenie
-bopper daughter's boy-friend.
He is like a lonely little winter robin.

We are that close to each other, I
Can nearly hear his heart beating.

I say something bland to make him grin,
But his glass eyes look past my side
-whiskers down
          the Shore Road street.
I am an Irish man
          and he is afraid
That I have come to kill him.

PADRAIC FIACC

INTERRUPTION TO A JOURNEY

The hare we had run over
Bounced about the road
On the springing curve
Of its spine.

Cornfields breathed in the darkness,
We were going through the darkness and
The breathing cornfields from one
Important place to another.

We broke the hare's neck
And made that place, for a moment,
The most important place there was,
Where a bowstring was cut
And a bow broken forever
That had shot itself through so many
Darknesses and cornfields.

It was left in that landscape.
It left us in another.

NORMAN MACCAIG

MOUSE'S NEST

I found a ball of grass among the hay
And progged it as I passed and went away;
And when I looked I fancied something stirred,
And turned agen and hoped to catch the bird –
When out an old mouse bolted in the wheats
With all her young ones hanging at her teats;
She looked so odd and so grotesque to me,
I ran and wondered what the thing could be,
And pushed the knapweed bunches where I stood;
Then the mouse hurried from the craking brood.
The young ones squeaked, and as I went away
She found her nest again among the hay.
The water o'er the pebbles scarce could run
And broad old cesspools glittered in the sun.

JOHN CLARE

Suggestions for assignments

1 The poems show a series of encounters which 'make that place for a moment the most important place there was'. The meetings are unexpected, pass quickly, but live in the mind.

Write your own piece, based on a real experience, or make one up. Decide who is meeting who or what, where they are, and what happens.

2 Consider the last two lines of the three poems in the anthology. Picture them in any way you wish, artwork as well as storyboard, sketch or diagram.

Write a commentary on your work, in which you explain your thinking, and also what your picturing cannot show. Describe what it was in the poems that made you come to your decisions.

The work you have already done on 'Travelling through the Dark' could be added to this assignment.